# Excel
## Basic Skills

KINDERGARTEN/ FOUNDATION

**K/F**

Ages 5–6

# English

Tanya Dalgleish



PASCAL PRESS

# Contents

# Introduction

The aim of the ***Excel*** **Basic Skills English** series is to build on and reinforce students' basic skills in English. Each book in the series supports the requirements of Australian Curriculum English at each year level.

The ***Excel*** **Basic Skills English** series consists of seven books, one for each year level, from Kindergarten/ Foundation to Year 6. The series is supported by other books in the ***Excel*** **Basic Skills** and **Advanced Skills** series.

## Structure of the book

This book contains:

- thirty carefully graded double-page units of teaching and learning activities. The first seven units focus on establishing familiarity with lower-case and upper-case letter shapes (e.g. developing visual discrimination through letter matching, naming letters, tracing letters and copying letters); learning to recognise the words for colours and numbers; developing an understanding of the sounds in words; developing an understanding about sequencing events in stories; matching pictures with words; and labelling pictures.
  - **Unit A** includes a sample text and deals with **Reading and Comprehension skills.**
  - **Unit B** deals with the language conventions of **Spelling, Vocabulary, Grammar and Punctuation**.
- four double-page **revision units** and four double-page **NAPLAN-style Tests**.

## How to use this book

- Students should complete one unit per week. A suggested plan would be to complete the Unit A page for the week on one day and the Unit B page on another day of the same week.
- At the end of a sequence of units students should undertake the applicable Revision units. If students find particular revision questions difficult they should revisit those areas in the previous sequence of units.
- After appropriate revision activities students should undertake the NAPLAN-style Test for those units. The revision work and testing should be completed on different days.

## How to use this book with the *Excel* Basic Skills Mathematics series

For a complete **weekly English and Mathematics program** use this book in conjunction with the ***Excel*** *Basic Skills Mathematics Kindergarten/Foundation* book. This way a student will have work set for four days a week—two days for English and two days for Mathematics.

## How to assess students' progress

- A template is included in each book of the series that outlines the knowledge and skills targeted by the questions in that book. (Please see page 6.)
- The questions move through the subtopics of English in exactly the same order in each book but as there are more questions and more complex material included in later years of the Kindergarten/Foundation to Year 6 continuum, the question numbers vary across the books.
- The results of the work undertaken in each unit can be recorded on the marking grids. Please see the example on page 4. The marking grids on pages 6 and 7 are an easy-to-use diagnostic tool that indicate where students' strengths and weaknesses lie in relation to specific areas of English. These results can be used to gather extra information about students' progress and their further revision needs.

## The *Excel* Basic Skills and Advanced Skills series

Further books to support students are available in the ***Excel*** **Basic Skills** and **Advanced Skills** series. (Please see the comprehensive list of ***Excel***/Pascal Press books on page 5.)

# The *Excel* step-by-step improvement plan

## Step 1

Read the introduction on page 3.

## Step 2

Read this page, along with the marking grids and question templates on pages 6 and 7.

- **Question templates**
  These outline the knowledge and skills targeted by the questions in the book.
  Remember that the questions move through the subtopics of English in exactly the same order in each unit of the book.
- **Marking grids**
  The results of the work undertaken in each unit can be recorded on the marking grids.
  These are an easy-to-use diagnostic tool that indicate where each student's strengths and weaknesses are in relation to specific areas of English.
  These results can be used to gather extra information about each student's progress and their further revision needs. For example, see the sample marking grid in the right-hand column:
  - If a student is consistently getting more than one in five questions wrong in any topic, they need help in this area.
  - When marking answers on the grid, simply mark incorrect answers with 'X' in the appropriate box. This will result in a graphical representation of areas needing further work. An example has been done above for Units 8 to 12. If a question has several parts, it should be counted as wrong if one or more mistakes are made.
  - Remember that you can identify exactly what type of questions a student is having difficulty with in a topic. For example, in the grid above the student is having difficulty with Reading and Comprehension inferring questions.

| | Literal | Literal | Literal | Literal | Inferring | Inferring |
|---|---|---|---|---|---|---|
| **Question** | **1** | **2** | **3** | **4** | **5** | **6** |
| **Unit 8** | | | | | X | |
| **Unit 9** | | | | | | X |
| **Unit 10** | | | | | | |
| **Unit 11** | | | | | | X |
| **Unit 12** | | | | | X | X |
| **Unit 13** | | | | | | |
| **Unit 14** | | | | | | |
| **Unit 15** | | | | | | |
| **Unit 16** | | | | | | |

This grid indicates that the student needs extra help and practice in inferring questions.

## Step 3

**Refer to page 5: *Excel* books to help you *get the results you want*!**

- Under each topic there is a comprehensive list of books in our range to help students.
  For example, if a student wants help with Reading and Comprehension inferring questions or is ready to move on to more challenging work the books shown at the top of the next page will help them.
  Each ***Excel*** book has a comprehensive contents page that will help you find the appropriate pages in the book to target the specific topic you want in each subject area.

# *Excel* books to help you *get the results you want!*

## Reading and Comprehension

*Excel*
Early Skills

9781877085857

*Excel*
Early Skills

9781877085864

*Excel*
Early Skills

9781741255874

*Excel*
Basic Skills Core

9781741255874

## Phonics

Reading Freedom

9781740200165

Reading Freedom

9781740200172

Reading Freedom

9781740208189

Reading Freedom

9781740290196

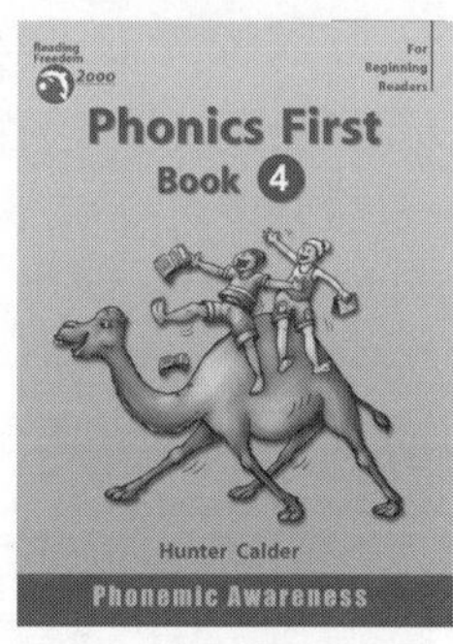


Reading Freedom

9781740200202

Reading Freedom

9781740200219

## Spelling and Vocabulary

*Excel*
Early Skills

9781877085840

*Excel*
Basic Skills Core

9781741255874

## Reading and Comprehension

QUESTION TEMPLATES

**1–4 Literal**
Answers to these questions are found directly in the text.

**5–6 Inferring**
Answers to these questions need to be worked out from clues in the text.

## Spelling

**1 Missing letters**
Students need to write the missing letters to make words used in the sample texts.

**2–3 Rhyming words**
Students need to identify rhyming words for words used in the texts.

**4 Initial sounds/Unscrambling words**
Students need to match pictures to initial sounds in text words or unscramble letters to make words from the texts.

**5 Phonemic awareness**
Students need to write initial sounds and/or listen for the number of sounds (phonemes) in words.

## Vocabulary

**6 Labels for pictures/Word meanings**
Students need to label pictures or use word meanings to identify words which don't belong in sets of three words.

## Grammar

**7 Nouns/Verbs/Adjectives/Conjunctions**
This question deals with proper and common nouns, action (doing) verbs, adjectives and conjunctions in compound sentences.

## Punctuation

**8 Sentences (capital letters, full stops and question marks)**
Students begin by copying simple sentences. They progress to unscrambling sentences so they make sense. Finally they learn to add capital letters for sentence beginnings and full stops or question marks to the ends of sentences.

## Reading and Comprehension

MARKING GRID

| | Literal | Literal | Literal | Literal | Inferring | Inferring |
|---|---|---|---|---|---|---|
| **Question** | 1 | 2 | 3 | 4 | 5 | 6 |
| **Unit 8** | | | | | | |
| **Unit 9** | | | | | | |
| **Unit 10** | | | | | | |
| **Unit 11** | | | | | | |
| **Unit 12** | | | | | | |
| **Unit 13** | | | | | | |
| **Unit 14** | | | | | | |
| **Unit 15** | | | | | | |
| **Unit 16** | | | | | | |
| **Unit 17** | | | | | | |
| **Unit 18** | | | | | | |
| **Unit 19** | | | | | | |
| **Unit 20** | | | | | | |
| **Unit 21** | | | | | | |
| **Unit 22** | | | | | | |
| **Unit 23** | | | | | | |
| **Unit 24** | | | | | | |
| **Unit 25** | | | | | | |
| **Unit 26** | | | | | | |
| **Unit 27** | | | | | | |
| **Unit 28** | | | | | | |
| **Unit 29** | | | | | | |
| **Unit 30** | | | | | | |
| **Question** | 1 | 2 | 3 | 4 | 5 | 6 |

**Units 1–7 focus on early literacy skills** and include activities that will help develop each student's sight vocabulary, knowledge of upper- and lower-case letter shapes, recognition of words and numerals for numbers, as well as words for basic colours. There are also activities to develop understandings about the sequencing of events in texts. **There is no marking grid for Units 1–7.** Please note that **Phonics** is covered under the subheading of Spelling in Units 8–30.

# Conventions of Language

| | Spelling | | | | | Vocabulary | Grammar | Punctuation |
|---|---|---|---|---|---|---|---|---|
| | Missing letters | Rhyming words | Rhyming words | Initial sounds / Unscrambling words | Phonemic awareness | Labels for pictures/ Word meanings | Nouns/ Verbs/ Adjectives/ Conjunctions | Sentences |
| **Question** | **1** | **2** | **3** | **4** | **5** | **6** | **7** | **8** |
| **Unit 8** | | | | | | | | |
| **Unit 9** | | | | | | | | |
| **Unit 10** | | | | | | | | |
| **Unit 11** | | | | | | | | |
| **Unit 12** | | | | | | | | |
| **Unit 13** | | | | | | | | |
| **Unit 14** | | | | | | | | |
| **Unit 15** | | | | | | | | |
| **Unit 16** | | | | | | | | |
| **Unit 17** | | | | | | | | |
| **Unit 18** | | | | | | | | |
| **Unit 19** | | | | | | | | |
| **Unit 20** | | | | | | | | |
| **Unit 21** | | | | | | | | |
| **Unit 22** | | | | | | | | |
| **Unit 23** | | | | | | | | |
| **Unit 24** | | | | | | | | |
| **Unit 25** | | | | | | | | |
| **Unit 26** | | | | | | | | |
| **Unit 27** | | | | | | | | |
| **Unit 28** | | | | | | | | |
| **Unit 29** | | | | | | | | |
| **Unit 30** | | | | | | | | |
| **Question** | **1** | **2** | **3** | **4** | **5** | **6** | **7** | **8** |

UNIT 1A

## The alphabet

| | | | | |
|---|---|---|---|---|
| a | b | c | d | e |
| f | g | h | i | j |
| k | l | m | n | o |
| p | q | r | s | t |
| u | v | w | x | y |
| z | | | | |

1. Point to the letters and say the letter names.
2. Trace the letters.
3. Colour the boxes of letters you can name.
4. How many letters can you name? ..............................

| a | b | c | d | e |
|---|---|---|---|---|
| f | g | h | i | j |
| k | l | m | n | o |
| p | q | r | s | t |
| u | v | w | x | y |
| z | | | | |

1 Trace the letters. Colour the letters in your first name.

2 Write your first name. ______________________

3 How many letters are in your name? ______________________

4 Say your name. How many sounds can you hear? ______________________

UNIT 2A

## Lower-case letters

| | | | | |
|---|---|---|---|---|
| x | e | w | d | v |
| f | y | k | o | j |
| z | b | u | a | n |
| p | d | l | r | b |
| g | q | a | h | s |
| t | m | c | n | i |

1. Trace the letters.
2. Point to the letters and say the letter names.
3. Colour the letters that are written twice.

Copy the letters on the lines below.

a c d e f o

g q s x y z

b h k m n r p

i j l t u v w

UNIT 3A

## Lower-case letters

| a | b | c | d | e |
|---|---|---|---|---|
| f | g | h | i | j |
| k | l | m | n | o |
| p | q | r | s | t |
| u | v | w | x | y |
| z | | | | |

1 Write the lower-case letters to match the upper-case letters shown in each box.

2 Write your full name.

UNIT 3B

Colour the lower-case letters. Link the lower-case letters to help the bee get back to its hive.

# Upper-case (capital) letters

| a | b | c | d | e |
|---|---|---|---|---|
| f | g | h | i | j |
| k | l | m | n | o |
| p | q | r | s | t |
| u | v | w | x | y |
| z | | | | |

1 Write the upper-case letters to match the lower-case letters in each box.

2 Write your name in upper-case letters.

Link the upper-case (capital) letters to help the wombat get back to its burrow.

## Predicting



1 In a story what could happen next? Draw it.

2 In a story what could happen next? Draw it.

## Matching letters

Circle the letters that match.

| | | |
|---|---|---|
| 1 | c | c a b c k c d |
| 2 | t | f t j t r t l |
| 3 | n | n m n r h m n |
| 4 | b | b p d g b q b |
| 5 | u | u w u i u v m |
| 6 | p | p q b c d g p |
| 7 | d | d b q p d g d |
| 8 | m | m n u m v r n |

## Numbers

Link the words to the pictures. Copy the words.

| | |
|---|---|
| one | |
| two | |
| three | |
| four | |
| five | |
| six | |
| seven | |
| eight | |
| nine | |
| ten | |

Link the words with the numerals. Draw strings from the balloons to the children.

## Colours

Link the pictures to the words for colours.

blue sea

green leaf

red rose

red

black

blue

white

brown

yellow

green

white cloud

black crow

brown bear

yellow sunflower

yellow banana

Draw a picture for each colour. Add a label to each picture.

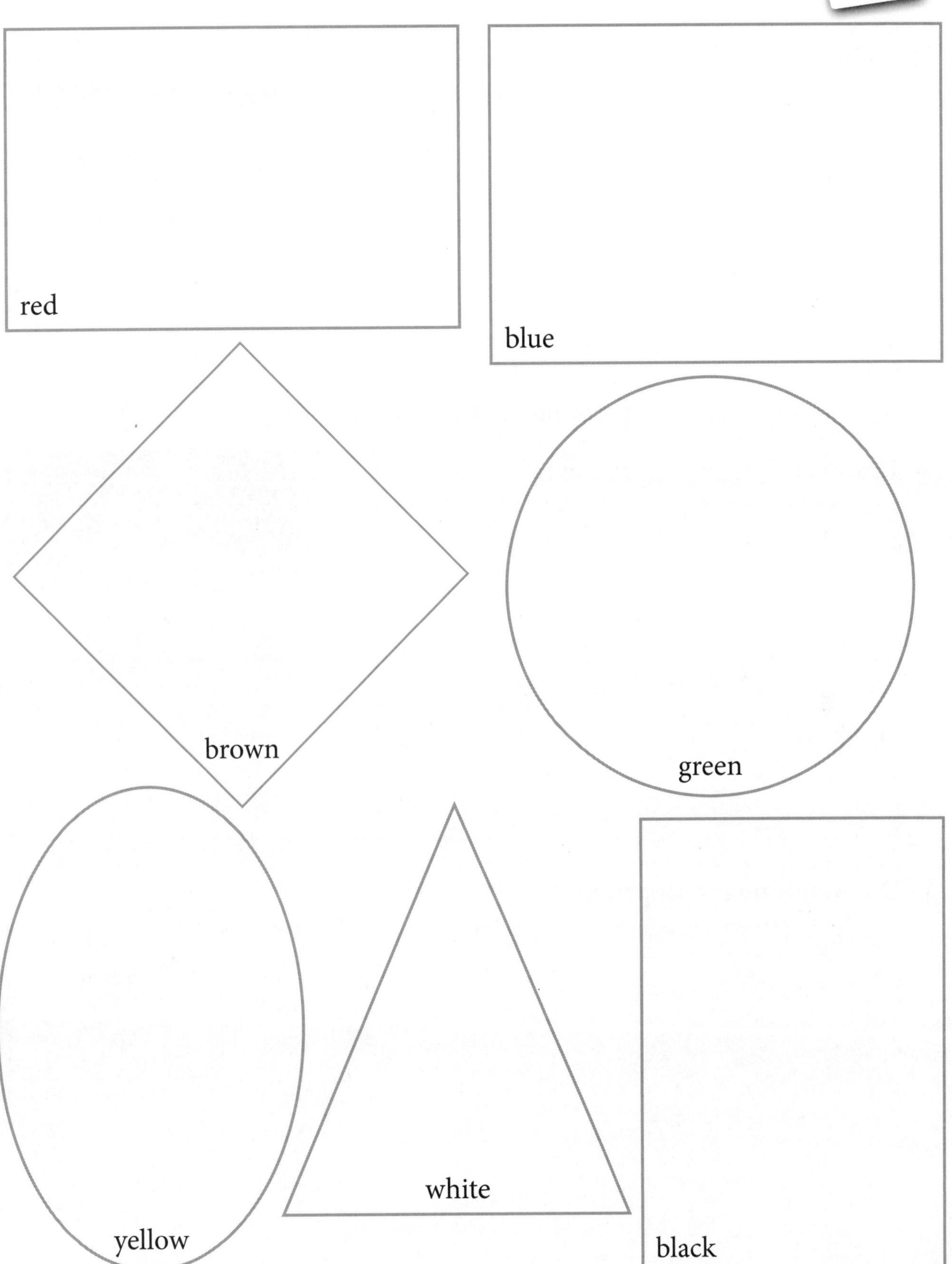

## Reading and Comprehension

1 Draw what might happen **next**.

2 Draw what might happen **next**.

3 Draw what might happen **next**.

4 Link the words to the numbers

0 1 2 3 4 5 6 7 8 9 10

six seven ten one two zero eight three nine four five

5 Write the words.

0 ______________________

1 ______________________

2 ______________________

3 ______________________

4 ______________________

5 ______________________

6 ______________________

7 ______________________

8 ______________________

9 ______________________

10 ______________________

6 Colour five circles yellow.

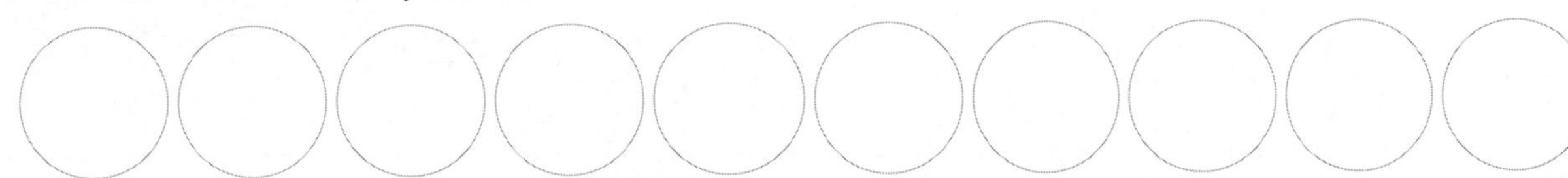

## Reading

1 Draw what might happen **next**.

2 Draw what might happen **next**.

3 Draw what might have happened **first**.

NAPLAN-STYLE

1

CONVENTIONS OF LANGUAGE TEST

1 Fill in the missing upper- or lower-case letters.

A ____ ____ b C ____ D ____ ____ e

____ f ____ g H ____ I ____ ____ j

____ k ____ l M ____ N ____ O ____

____ p Q ____ R ____ ____ s T ____

____ u V ____ ____ w ____ x Y ____

____ z

2 Write words that you know. Read them to a partner.

## Reading and Comprehension

# Cat

It is a cat.

It can sit.

1 Circle the correct word from the text. It is a ______________.

**A** hat **B** cat **C** rat

2 Which picture matches the text? Colour the correct answer.

**A**  **B**  **C** 

3 The cat can sit. ☐ yes ☐ no

4 The cat can hat. ☐ yes ☐ no

5 Circle what might happen next in the text.

**A**  **B**  **C** 

6 What can a cat do?
Write or draw a picture.

## Spelling

1 Write the missing letters to make words from the text.

**A** c ........ t

**B** c ........ n

**C** s ........ t

2 Which word rhymes with **cat**?

**A** sat **B** car **C** can

3 Which word rhymes with **sit**?

**A** sat **B** hit **C** pot

4 Draw a line to join the first sound to the picture.

**A** c

**B** h

**C** r

5 Say the name. Write the letter that makes the first sound.

**A** ........

**B** ........

**C** ........

## Vocabulary

6 Link the **correct** label to the picture.

**A** cat

**B** dog

**C** hop

## Grammar

7 Nouns are words for people, places, animals and things. Add a noun to the sentence.

This is a ........ .

## Punctuation

8 Copy the sentence correctly.
It is a cat.

........

........

........

## Reading and Comprehension

# Dog

This is my dog, Tig.

I love my dog.

1 Circle the correct word from the text. This is my ____________.

A dig B dad C dog

2 Which picture matches the text? Colour the correct answer.

A

B 

C 

3 The dog can sit. ☐ yes ☐ no

4 The dog is Dad. ☐ yes ☐ no

5 Circle what might happen next in the text.

A 

B 

C 

6 What can a dog do?
Write or draw a picture.

## Spelling

1 Write the missing letters to make words from the text.

**A** d ........ g

**B** m ........

**C** lov ........

2 Which word rhymes with **dog**?

**A** bag **B** dad **C** log

3 Which word rhymes with **Tig**?

**A** dig **B** dug **C** dog

4 Draw a line to join the first sound to the picture.

**A** d

**B** c

**C** s

5 Say the name. Write the letter that makes the first sound.

**A** ........

**B** ........

**C** ........

## Vocabulary

6 Link the **correct** label to the picture.

**A** This dog can dig.

**B** This dog can sit.

**C** This is a cat.

## Grammar

7 Nouns are words for people, places, animals and things. Add a noun to the sentence.

This is a ........ .

## Punctuation

8 Copy the sentence correctly.
This is my dog.

........

........

........

## Reading and Comprehension

### Ant

This is an ant. It has six legs. It bit me!

1 Circle the correct word from the text. This is an ____________.

**A** alligator **B** an **C** ant

2 Which picture matches the text? Colour the correct answer.

**A**  **B** 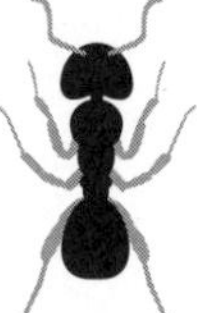 **C** 

3 The ant has six legs. ☐ yes ☐ no

4 Ants have six legs. ☐ yes ☐ no

5 Circle what might happen next in the text.

**A**  **B**  **C** 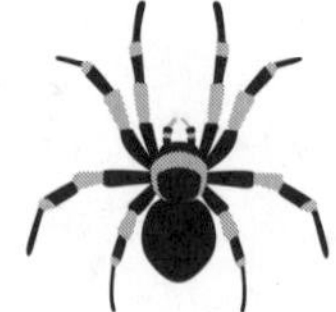

6 Draw an ant on the hat.

## Spelling

1 Write the missing letters to make words from the text.

**A** a ________ t

**B** le ________

**C** bi ________

2 Which word rhymes with **bit**?

**A** big **B** bin **C** sit

3 Which word rhymes with **an**?

**A** man **B** bit **C** ant

4 Draw a line to join the first sound to the picture.

**A** d

**B** a

**C** c

5 Say the name. Write the letter that makes the first sound.

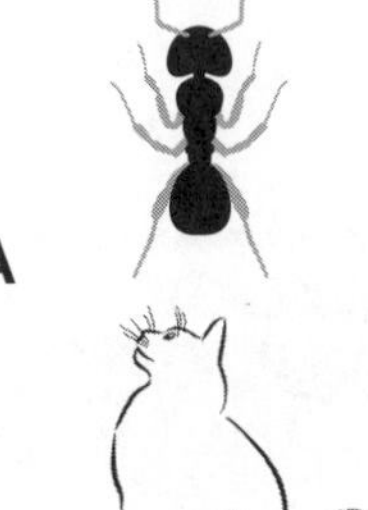

**A** ________

**B** ________

**C** ________

## Vocabulary

6 Link the **correct** label to the picture.

**A** A dog can dig.

**B** A cat can sit.

**C** Ants can dig.

## Grammar

7 Circle the correct noun.

This is a (fox / box / ant).

## Punctuation

8 Copy the sentence correctly.
An ant bit me!

________

________

________

## Reading and Comprehension

# Pig

Here is one pig.

It can dig in the mud.

1 Circle the correct word from the text. Here is one ______________ in the mud.

**A** pigs **B** pig **C** dog

2 Which picture matches the text? Colour the correct answer.

**A**  **B**  **C** 

3 A pig can mud. ☐ yes ☐ no

4 The pig can dig. ☐ yes ☐ no

5 Circle what might happen next in the text.

**A**  **B**  **C** 

6 Draw an animal that digs.

## Spelling

1 Write the missing letters to make words from the text.

A m ........ d

B p ........ g

C d ........ g

2 Which word rhymes with **pig**?

A pot B dog C dig

3 Which word rhymes with **pot**?

A top B got C pig

4 Draw a line to join the first sound to the picture.

A m

B d

C g

5 Say the name. Write the letter that makes the first sound.

A  ........

B  ........

C  ........

## Vocabulary

6 Link the **correct** label to the picture.

A A dog can dig.

B A cat can sit.

C A pig can sit.

## Grammar

7 Verbs can tell actions.
Write a verb for what a pig can do.

A pig can ........ .

## Punctuation

8 Copy the sentence correctly.
A pig can dig.

........

........

........

## Reading and Comprehension

### Ten

This is ten.

I have ten fingers.

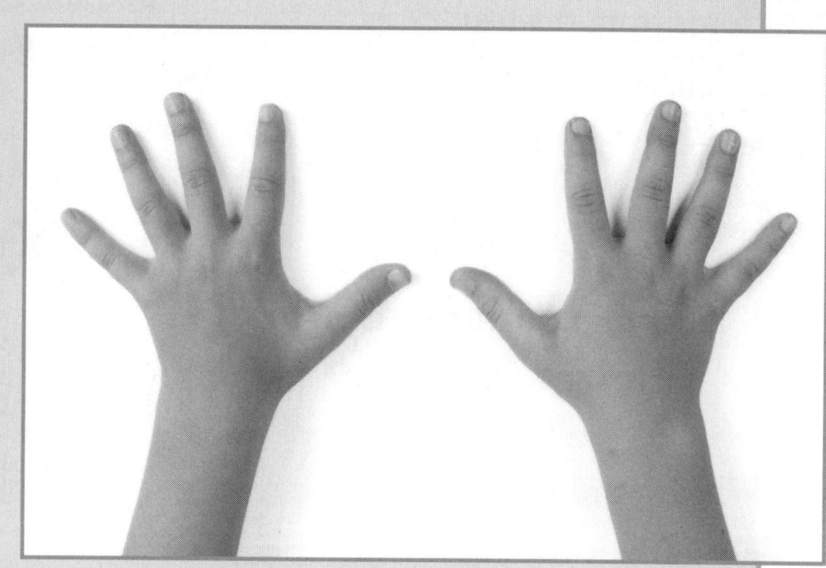

1. Circle the correct word from the text. I have ________________ fingers.

   **A** hen  **B** top  **C** ten

2. Which picture matches the text? Colour the correct answer.

   **A**   **B**   **C** 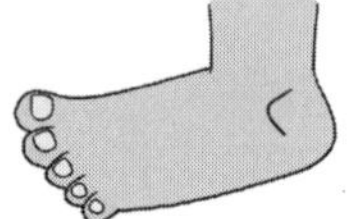

3. I have only two fingers. ☐ yes ☐ no

4. I have ten fingers. ☐ yes ☐ no

5. Circle what might happen next in the text.

   **A** 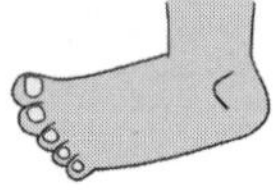  **B** 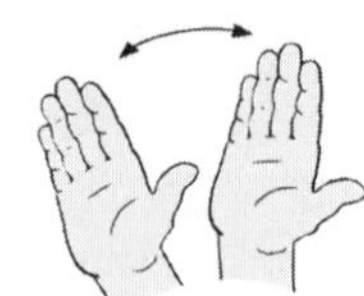  **C** 

6. Draw something your fingers can do.

## Spelling

1 Write the missing letters to make words from the text.

A t ______ n

B hav ______

C f ______ ngers

2 Which word rhymes with **ten**?

A top B pen C net

3 Which word rhymes with **ten**?

A two B tent C men

4 Draw a line to join the first sound to the picture.

A t

B n

C p

5 Say the name. Write the letter that makes the first sound.

A ______

B ______

C ______

## Vocabulary

6 Link the **correct** label to the picture.

A This is a duck.

B This is big.

C This is ten.

## Grammar

7 Draw ten pencils in the cup.

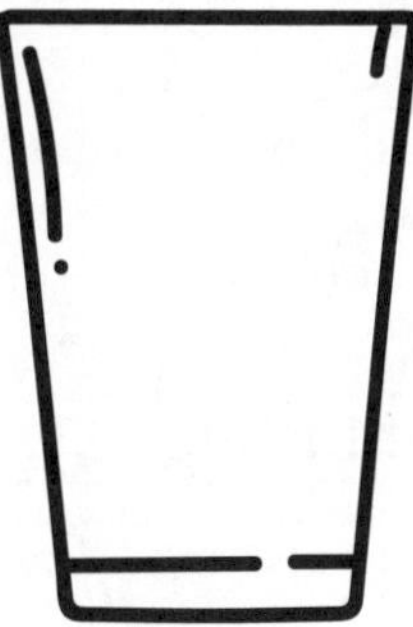

## Punctuation

8 Copy the sentence correctly.
I have ten fingers.

______

______

______

## Reading and Comprehension

# Big

This elephant is big. It has a trunk.

1 Circle the correct word from the text. This elephant is ______________.

**A** long **B** bad **C** big

2 Which picture matches the text? Colour the correct answer.

**A**  **B**  **C** 

3 The elephant is big. ☐ yes ☐ no

4 It has a trunk. ☐ yes ☐ no

5 Circle what might happen next in the text.

**A**  **B**  **C** 

6 Draw an elephant in mud.

## Spelling

1 Write the missing letters to make words from the text.

A b ........ g

B elephan ........

C h ........ s

2 Which word rhymes with **big**?

A has B pig C baby

3 Which word rhymes with **big**?

A bog B dog C dig

4 Draw a line to join the first sound to the picture.

A b

B t

C e

5 Say the name. Write the letter that makes the first sound.

A

B

C

## Vocabulary

6 Link the **correct** label to the picture.

A This pig is little.

B This elephant is little.

C This is a little dog.

## Grammar

7 Verbs can tell actions.
Write a verb for what an elephant can do.

An elephant can ........ .

## Punctuation

8 Copy the sentence correctly.
This elephant is big.

........

........

........

## Reading and Comprehension

# Eggs

I can see three eggs in the nest. They are white.

1 Circle the correct word from the text. I can see three ..................................... .

**A** egs **B** egg **C** eggs

2 Which picture matches the text? Colour the correct answer.

**A**  B  **C** 

3 There are three eggs. ☐ yes ☐ no

4 The eggs are not in the nest. ☐ yes ☐ no

5 Circle what might happen next in the text.

**A**  **B**  **C** 

6 Draw two eggs in a nest.

## Spelling

1 Write the missing letters to make words from the text.

A ________ ggs

B se ________

C n ________ st

2 Which word rhymes with **see**?

A eggs B can C three

3 Which word rhymes with **nest**?

A best B nice C eggs

4 Draw a line to join the first sound to the picture.

A n

B s

C e

5 Say the name. Write the letter that makes the first sound.

A ________

B ________

C ________

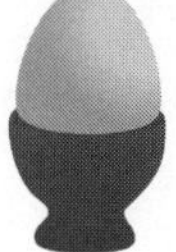

## Vocabulary

6 Link the **correct** label to the picture.

A This is an egg.

B This is a big tree.

C This is a nest.

## Grammar

7 Nouns are words for people, places, animals and things. Add a noun to the sentence.

A bird is in the ________.

## Punctuation

8 Copy the sentence correctly.
I see three eggs.

________

________

________

UNIT 15A

## Reading and Comprehension

# Fat and fluffy

This cat is fat and fluffy. Its name is Fred.

1 Circle the correct word from the text. This cat is ______________.

**A** fit **B** cat **C** fat

2 Which picture matches the text? Colour the correct answer.

**A** **B** **C**

3 The cat is fluffy. ☐ yes ☐ no

4 Its name is Fred. ☐ yes ☐ no

5 Circle what might happen next in the text.

**A** **B** **C**

6 Draw something the cat might like to do.

## Spelling

1 Write the missing letters to make words from the text.

A f ______ t

B nam ______

C Thi ______

2 Which word rhymes with **Ted**?

A fat B cat C Fred

3 Which word rhymes with **cat**?

A fluffy B fat C This

4 Draw a line to join the first sound to the picture.

A f

B m

C c

5 Say the name. Write the letter that makes the first sound.

A ______

B ______

C ______

## Vocabulary

6 Link the **correct** label to the picture.

© Anna Dudko | Dreamstime Stock Photos

A The cat is fat.

B This is a fat rat.

C Fred is a rat.

## Grammar

7 People's names and pet names are proper nouns. A proper noun begins with a capital letter.

What is the cat's name?

______

## Punctuation

8 Copy the sentence correctly.
This is a fat cat.

______

______

______

# Reading and Comprehension

Add a word from the box to each sentence.

| ant | pig | cat | dog |
|---|---|---|---|

1 It is a ________________.

2 This is a ________________.

3 This is an ________________. It bit me.

4 A ________________ can dig.

Add a word from the box to each sentence.

| ten | nest | fluffy | big |
|---|---|---|---|

5 This is ________________.

6 This elephant is ________________.

7 I can see a ________________.

8 This cat is ________________.

# Answers

### Unit 1A page 8

Answers will vary; parent/teacher to check

### Unit 1B page 9

Answers will vary; parent/teacher to check

### Unit 2A page 10

**3.** b, a, d, n

### Unit 2B page 11

parent/teacher to check

### Unit 3A page 12

parent/teacher to check

### Unit 3B page 13

**1.** Colour a, g, d, e, f, e, m, n.
**2.** Link a, g, d, e, f, e, m, n.

### Unit 4A page 14

parent/teacher to check

### Unit 4B page 15

Link A, H, J, F, B, C, E, K, L, M, Z.

### Unit 5A page 16

**1.** Parent/teacher to check, e.g. the child in the photo might lose the balloons or the child might get carried into the sky.
**2.** Parent/teacher to check, e.g. the child might catch a fish or fall into the water.

### Unit 5B page 17

| | | |
|---|---|---|
| **1.** | c | ⓒ a b ⓒ k ⓒ d |
| **2.** | t | f ⓣ j ⓣ r ⓣ l |
| **3.** | n | ⓝ m ⓝ r h m ⓝ |
| **4.** | b | ⓑ p d g ⓑ q ⓑ |
| **5.** | u | ⓤ w ⓤ i ⓤ v m |
| **6.** | p | ⓟ q b c d g ⓟ |
| **7.** | d | ⓓ b q p ⓓ g ⓓ |
| **8.** | m | ⓜ n u ⓜ v r n |

### Unit 6A page 18

| | |
|---|---|
| zero | |
| one | |
| two | |
| three | |
| four | |
| five | |
| six | |
| seven | |
| eight | |
| nine | |
| ten | |

### Unit 6B page 19

parent/teacher to check (Note: Balloons 5, 7 and 8 will have no match. Children two and four will have two balloons each.)

### Unit 7A page 20

yellow: yellow banana, yellow sunflower
green: green leaf
brown: brown bear
black: black crow
red: red rose
white: white cloud
blue: blue sea

### Unit 7B page 21

Parent/teacher to check.

### Revision 1 pages 22-23

**1.** Parent/teacher to check, e.g. the child might cut his fingers.
**2.** Parent/teacher to check, e.g. the child might kick a goal or trip over.
**3.** Parent/teacher to check, e.g. the monkey might fall off the branch.
**4.** and **5.** 0—zero, one—1, two—2, three—3, four—4, five—5, six—6, seven—7, eight—8, nine—9, ten—10.
**6.** ●●●●●○○○○○

# Answers

## NAPLAN-style Reading Test 1 page 24

1. Parent/teacher to check, e.g. the dog might get taken for a walk.
2. Parent/teacher to check, e.g. the child will be very happy with the gift in the box.
3. Parent/teacher to check, e.g. the child is standing on the stairs.

## NAPLAN-style Conventions of Language Test 1 page 25

1. A a / B b / C c / D d
   E e / F f / G g / H h
   I i / J j / K k / L l / M m
   N n / O o / P p / Q q
   R r / S s / T t / U u / V v
   W w / X x / Y y / Z z
2. parent/teacher to check

## Unit 8A page 26

1. B.
2. B.
3. yes
4. no
5. A.
6. Parent/teacher to check, e.g. a cat sleeping/ chasing a mouse/ climbing a tree.

## Unit 8B page 27

1. A. a B. a C. i
2. A.
3. B.
4. 

5. A. c B. c C. c
6. A.
7. cat
8. It is a cat.

## Unit 9A page 28

1. C.
2. C.
3. yes
4. no
5. A.
6. parent/teacher to check

## Unit 9B page 29

1. A. o B. y C. e
2. C.
3. A.
4. 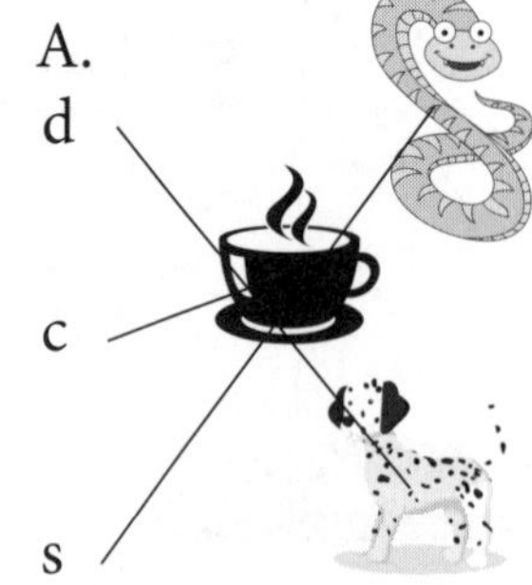

5. A. d B. c C. a
6. A.
7. dog
8. This is my dog.

## Unit 10A page 30

1. C.
2. B.
3. yes
4. yes
5. A.
6. parent/teacher to check

## Unit 10B page 31

1. A. n B. g C. t
2. C.
3. A.
4. 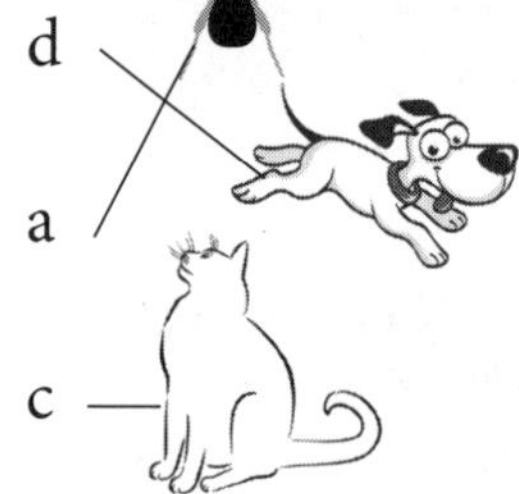

5. A. a B. c C. t
6. C.
7. box
8. An ant bit me!

## Unit 11A page 32

1. B.
2. B.
3. no
4. yes
5. A.
6. parent/teacher to check

# Answers

## Unit 11B page 33

1. A. u B. i C. i
2. C.
3. B.
4. m

   d

   g

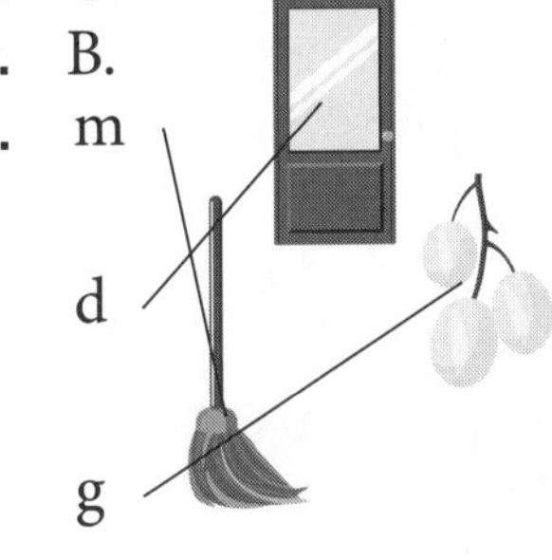

5. A. m
   (Note: The picture shows a mop so *m* is correct; however, children might suggest the item is a broom in which case *b* is correct.)
   B. d C. p
6. C.
7. dig
8. A pig can dig.

## Unit 12A page 34

1. C.
2. B.
3. no
4. yes
5. B.
6. parent/teacher to check

## Unit 12B page 35

1. A. e B. e C. i
2. B.
3. C.
4. t

   n

   p

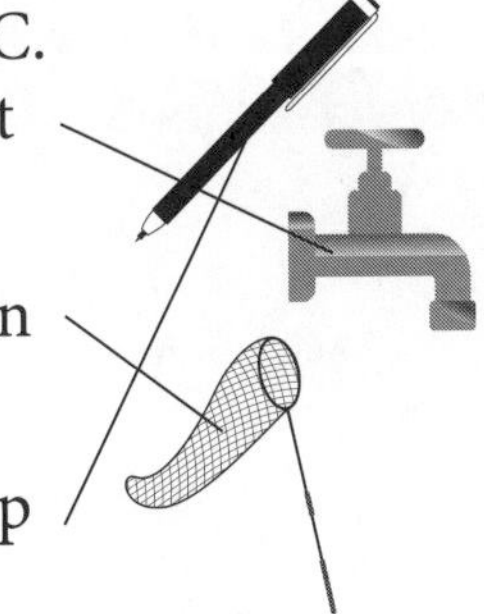

5. A. m
   (Note: The picture shows a mop so *m* is correct; however, children might suggest the item is a broom in which case *b* is correct.)
   B. d C. p
6. C.
7. parent/teacher to check
8. I have ten fingers.

## Unit 13A page 36

1. C.
2. A.
3. yes
4. yes
5. C.
6. parent/teacher to check

## Unit 13B page 37

1. A. i B. t C. a
2. B.
3. C.
4. b

   t

   e

5. A. e B. t C. c
6. B.
7. e.g. run, dig
8. This elephant is big.

## Unit 14A page 38

1. C.
2. B.
3. yes
4. no
5. A.
6. parent/teacher to check

## Unit 14B page 39

1. A. e B. e C. e
2. C.
3. A.
4. n

   s

   e

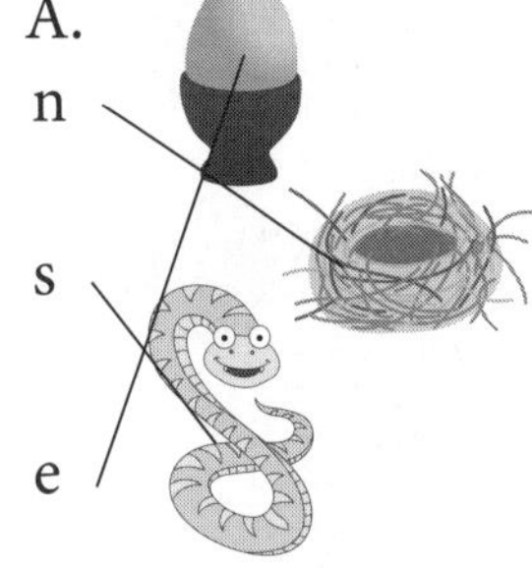

5. A. s B. n C. e
6. C.
7. nest
8. I see three eggs.

## Unit 15A page 40

1. C.
2. C.
3. yes
4. yes
5. C. (Note: Students can infer that the fat cat likes to eat and is not very active so C is the best answer.)
6. parent/teacher to check

# Answers

## Unit 15B page 41

1. A. a  B. e  C. s
2. C.
3. B.
4. f

m

c

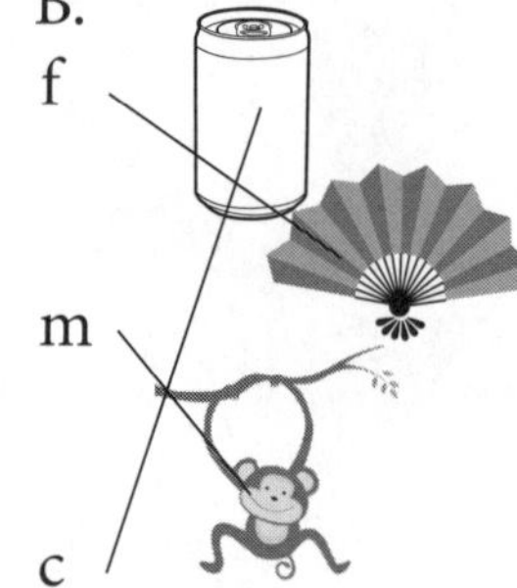

5. A. m  B. f  C. c
6. B.
7. Fred
8. This is a fat cat.

## Revision 2 pages 42–43

1. cat
2. pig
3. ant
4. dog
5. ten
6. big
7. nest
8. fluffy
9. cat
10. dog
11. pig
12. bit
13. rat
14. ten
15. big
16. dig

## NAPLAN-style Reading Test 2 page 44

1. C.
2. C.
3. B.
4. A.
5. A.
6. B.

## NAPLAN-style Conventions of Language Test 2 page 45

1. A. o  B. i  C. a
2. C.
3. C.
4. A, B, A.
5. pig
6. B.
7. dog
8. One dog is big.

## Unit 16A page 46

1. B.
2. B.
3. Nan
4. Mum
5. parent/teacher to check
6. A.

## Unit 16B page 47

1. A. s  B. s  C. n
2. C.
3. A.
4. A. fun  B. helps
   C. Mum
5. A. 4  B. 3  C. 3
6. C.
7. Mum
8. Nan has fun.

## Unit 17A page 48

1. C.
2. A.
3. jump
4. kangaroos/brown
5. parent/teacher to check
6. parent/teacher to check

## Unit 17B page 49

1. A. e  B. p  C. y
2. B.
3. A.
4. A. are  B. two
   C. They
5. A. 4  B. 4  C. 4
6. C or B. (Note: C is correct because *kangaroo* is a noun while *run* and *jump* are verbs. B is also correct because a kangaroo can jump. It does not run.)
7. kangaroos
8. They are brown.

## Unit 18A page 50

1. B.
2. B.
3. jump
4. nine
5. parent/teacher to check
6. yes

# Answers

## Unit 18B page 51

1. A. e B. y C. k
2. B.
3. A.
4. A. look B. happy
   C. nine/Nine
5. A. 3 B. 4 C. 3
6. B.
7. Answers will vary, e.g. children.
8. It looks fun.

## Unit 19A page 52

1. B.
2. A.
3. kiss
4. loves
5. parent/teacher to check
6. yes

## Unit 19B page 53

1. A. i B. u C. s
2. B.
3. C.
4. A. kiss B. loves
   C. funny
5. A. 3 B. 2 C. 3
6. A. (Note: A is correct because *Lindy* is a name (proper noun) while *funny* and *little* are words that describe.)
7. sister/Sam
8. Lindy has a sister.

## Unit 20A page 54

1. C.
2. A.
3. name
4. run
5. parent/teacher to check
6. yes

## Unit 20B page 55

1. A. u B. a C. e
2. B.
3. A.
4. A. run B. fast
   C. name
5. A. 3 B. 3 C. 3
6. B.
7. dog/Red
8. Red can run.

## Unit 21A page 56

1. C.
2. A.
3. job
4. Wednesday
5. parent/teacher to check
6. yes (Note: You can infer from the playful photo that the vet likes his job.)

## Unit 21B page 57

1. A. e B. k C. b
2. B.
3. C.
4. A. took B. see C. job
5. A. 3 B. 3 C. 3
6. C.
7. Coco
8. A vet has a good job.

## Unit 22A page 58

1. C.
2. A.
3. sat
4. bug
5. parent/teacher to check
6. parent/teacher to check

## Unit 22B page 59

1. A. e B. e C. u
2. C.
3. B.
4. A. eat B. bug C. web
5. A. 3 B. 3 C. 3
6. B or C. (Note: B is correct because the text includes *bug* and *web* but not *ant*. C could also be correct because *bug* and *ant* are animals or living things and *web* is not an animal.)
7. Spider/spider/hungry
8. It needed a bug.

## Unit 23A page 60

1. C.
2. B.
3. good/muffins
4. banana/yummy
5. parent/teacher to check
6. yes (Note: You can infer that the writer likes bananas based on the writer's judgement that the banana muffins are yummy.)

# Answers

## Unit 23B page 61

1. A. d B. oo C. e
2. C.
3. B.
4. A. made B. yum C. muffins
5. A. 3 B. 3 C. 3
6. C.
7. muffin/yummy/muffins
8. We made muffins.

## Revision 3 pages 62–63

1. sisters
2. Kangaroos
3. jump
4. help
5. web
6. good
7. run
8. vet
9. web
10. Yum
11. fun
12. run
13. two
14. look
15. kiss
16. vet

## NAPLAN-style Reading Test 3 page 64

1. A.
2. C.
3. C.
4. C.
5. A.
6. yes

## NAPLAN-style Conventions of Language Test 3 page 65

1. A. a B. u C. e
2. A.
3. B.
4. A. name B. jump C. fast
5. A. 3 B. 4 C. 3
6. A.
7. A. Scarlet or sister B. Kangaroo or rat
8. A rat is a good pet.

## Unit 24A page 66

1. B.
2. C.
3. cat
4. jump
5. parent/teacher to check
6. B.

## Unit 24B page 67

1. A. x B. x C. y
2. B.
3. B.
4. A. box B. play C. out
5. A. 3 B. 4 C. 4
6. C.
7. jumps
8. Foxy likes to play.

## Unit 25A page 68

1. C.
2. A.
3. white
4. zoom
5. yes
6. A.

## Unit 25B page 69

1. A. e B. o C. i
2. C.
3. B.
4. A. zero B. zoo C. zoom
5. A. 2 B. 3 C. 4
6. zebra
7. black, white
8. Zed is for zero.

# Answers

## Unit 26A page 70

1. A.
2. B.
3. duck
4. quiet
5. no
6. quiet

## Unit 26B page 71

1. A. qu B. qu C. e
2. B.
3. A.
4. A. quick B. quack C. duck
5. A. 3 B. 3 C. 4
6. C.
7. but
8. A snail is not quick.

## Unit 27A page 72

1. A.
2. C.
3. rules
4. Keep
5. no
6. C.

## Unit 27B page 73

1. A. o B. o C. k
2. B.
3. B.
4. A. walk B. grass C. rules
5. A 4 B. 3 C. 3
6. C.
7. and
8. Can you follow the rules?

## Unit 28A page 74

1. B.
2. A.
3. funny
4. read
5. no
6. B.

## Unit 28B page 75

1. A. u B. e C. o
2. C.
3. A.
4. A. book B. thank C. helping
5. A. 3 B. 4 C. 3
6. C.
7. because
8. Thank you for the book.

## Unit 29A page 76

1. C.
2. C.
3. soap
4. germs
5. yes
6. A.

## Unit 29B page 77

1. A. a B. a C. a
2. B.
3. C.
4. A. please B. hands C. wash
5. A. 3 B. 4 C. 3
6. B.
7. so (*and* could also be considered correct)
8. Did you wash with soap?

## Unit 30A page 78

1. A.
2. A.
3. worms
4. scraps/food
5. yes
6. B.

## Unit 30B page 79

1. A. d B. a C. a
2. C.
3. B.
4. A. house B. food C. worms
5. A. 3 B. 4 C. 3
6. C.
7. and
8. Do you recycle food scraps?

# Answers

## Revision 4 pages 80–81

1. Keep
2. Quack
3. Zebras
4. boxes
5. paper
6. soap
7. book
8. eat
9. box
10. zoom
11. quick
12. funny
13. Wash
14. rid
15. glass
16. paper

## NAPLAN-style Reading Test 4 page 82

1. C.
2. A.
3. C.
4. B.
5. yes
6. yes (Note: Nathan says he likes rules and gives reasons. You can infer that he follows the rules.)

## NAPLAN-style Conventions of Language Test 4 page 83

1. A. e B. e C. y
2. C.
3. A.
4. A. school B. rules C. read
5. A. 3 B. 4 C. 3
6. B. (Note: The text links *safe* and *happy*.)
7. Parent/teacher to check, e.g. Nathan at school/ Nathan.
8. Nathan reads every day.

## Spelling, Vocabulary, Grammar and Punctuation

Write the missing words.
Using a different colour for each word, colour in the letters that make the words.
The first one has been done for you. Use every letter once.

| | | | | | |
|---|---|---|---|---|---|
| 9 | © Dimitar Dimitrov \| Dreamstime Stock Photos | This is a _c_ _a_ _t_. | b | o | t |
| 10 | | This is a ___ ___ ___. | c | a | g |
| 11 | | This is a ___ ___ ___. | d | e | n |
| 12 | | This ant ___ ___ ___ me. | d | a | g |
| 13 | © Anna Dudko \| Dreamstime Stock Photos | This is a ___ ___ ___. | p | i | t |
| 14 | | This is ___ ___ ___. | b | i | t |
| 15 | | This is ___ ___ ___. | t | i | g |
| 16 | | This dog can ___ ___ ___. | r | i | g |

## Reading

# Three dogs

I can see three dogs. One dog is big. Its name is Meg.

Two dogs are not big. They are little. One is Bob and one is Ted.

The three dogs can sit. One of the little dogs loves to dig. I love dogs.

1 The big dog's name is

**A** Bob.

**B** Ted.

**C** Meg.

2 How many dogs are there?

**A** one

**B** two

**C** three

3 How many little dogs are there?

**A** one

**B** two

**C** three

4 How many big dogs are there?

**A** one

**B** two

**C** three

5 Are the dogs pets?

**A** yes

**B** no

6 Does the big dog love to dig?

**A** yes

**B** no

## Spelling

1 Write the missing letters to make words from the text.

**A** d ____ g  **B** b ____ g  **C** c ____ n

2 Circle the word that rhymes with **can**.

**A** dog  **B** cat  **C** man

3 Circle the word that rhymes with **sit**.

**A** rat  **B** sat  **C** pit

4 Circle the letter that makes the first sound for each word.

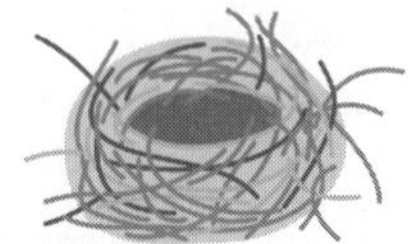

**A** m **B** n **C** c  **A** m **B** n **C** d  **A** a **B** m **C** n

5 Write the word for the picture.

______________________________

## Vocabulary

6 Link the **correct** label to the picture.

**A** This is a white rat.

**B** This is a fat rat.

**C** This is a dig rat.

© Anna Dudko | Dreamstime Stock Photos

## Grammar

7 Circle the noun.
dog bit little

## Punctuation

8 Copy the sentence.
One dog is big.

______________________________

## Reading and Comprehension

# Help

Mum helps Nan

on the computer.

Nan has fun.

1. Circle the correct word from the text.
   Mum ______________ Nan on the computer.
   - **A** help
   - **B** helps
   - **C** Nan

2. Circle the sentence that matches the picture.
   - **A** Nan can run.
   - **B** Nan has fun.
   - **C** Nan can dig.

3. Write a word from the text.
   Who is on the computer?

   ______________________________

4. Write a word from the text.
   Who helps?

   ______________________________

5. Draw what might happen next in the text.

6. Which word tells you Nan likes the computer?
   - **A** fun
   - **B** Nan
   - **C** help

## Spelling

1 Write the missing letters to make words from the text.

**A** help ..........

**B** ha ..........

**C** fu ..........

2 Which word rhymes with **Nan**?

**A** nag

**B** not

**C** can

3 Which word rhymes with **fun**?

**A** run

**B** hit

**C** pit

4 Unscramble the letters to make words from the text.

**A** nuf ..........

**B** pelhs ..........

**C** mMu ..........

5 Say the word. How many sounds can you hear?

**A** help ..........

**B** Mum ..........

**C** fun ..........

## Vocabulary

6 Which word does **not** belong?

**A** good

**B** fun

**C** bad

## Grammar

7 Write a noun on the line.

This is .......................... .

## Punctuation

8 Copy the sentence correctly on the lines.

Nan has fun.

..........................

..........................

..........................

Reading and Comprehension

# Kangaroos

Here are two

kangaroos.

They are brown.

Kangaroos can jump.

1 Circle the correct word from the text.
They can ______________.

A two

B kangaroo

C jump

2 Circle the sentence that matches the picture.

A Here are two kangaroos.

B Here are three kangaroos.

C Here is a kangaroo.

3 Write a word from the text.
What can a kangaroo do?

______________

4 Write a word from the text.
What are they?

______________

5 Draw what might happen next in the text.

6 Do you like kangaroos?

☐ yes

☐ no

## Spelling

1 Write the missing letters to make words from the text.

**A** ar ______

**B** jum ______

**C** The ______

2 Which word rhymes with **brown**?

**A** bring

**B** down

**C** row

3 Which word rhymes with **jump**?

**A** pump

**B** look

**C** happy

4 Unscramble the letters to make words from the text.

**A** aer ______

**B** tow ______

**C** Thye ______

5 Say the word. How many sounds can you hear?

**A** jump ______

**B** dump ______

**C** pump ______

## Vocabulary

6 Which word does **not** belong?

**A** jump

**B** run

**C** kangaroo

## Grammar

7 Write a noun on the line.

Two ______

## Punctuation

8 Write the sentence correctly on the lines.

| brown. | They | are |
|---|---|---|

______

______

______

## Reading and Comprehension

# Jump

Nine children can jump. They look happy.

It looks fun.

1. Circle the correct word from the text.
   They look ______________.
   - **A** jump
   - **B** happy
   - **C** children

2. Circle the sentence that matches the picture.
   - **A** Here are no children.
   - **B** Nine can jump.
   - **C** Here is a child.

3. Write a word from the text.
   What can children do?

   ______________

   ______________

4. Write a word from the text.
   How many children are there?

   ______________

5. Draw something children can do.

6. Are the nine children happy?
   - ☐ yes
   - ☐ no

## Spelling

1 Write the missing letters to make words from the text.

**A** Nin ______

**B** happ ______

**C** loo ______

2 Which word rhymes with **look**?

**A** cool

**B** cook

**C** loot

3 Which word rhymes with **jump**?

**A** lump

**B** look

**C** happy

4 Unscramble the letters to make words from the text.

**A** kool ______

**B** yapph ______

**C** neni ______

5 Say the word. How many sounds can you hear?

**A** look ______

**B** happy ______

**C** fun ______

## Vocabulary

6 Which word does **not** belong?

**A** happy

**B** sad

**C** good

## Grammar

7 Write a noun on the line.

Nine ______

## Punctuation

8 Write the sentence correctly on the lines.

| fun. | It | looks |
|---|---|---|

______

______

______

## Reading and Comprehension

# Sisters

Lindy loves her

little sister, Sam.

She loves to kiss

Sam. Sam is funny.

1 Circle the correct word from the text.
Lindy is Sam's ______________.

**A** kiss

**B** sister

**C** children

2 Circle the words that match the picture.

**A** Lindy and Sam

**B** This is Lindy.

**C** Here is a sister.

3 Write a word from the text.

Lindy loves to ______________ Sam.

4 Write a word from the text.

Lindy ______________ Sam.

5 Draw something Lindy can do with Sam.

6 Is Lindy a good sister?

☐ yes

☐ no

## Spelling

1 Write the missing letters to make words from the text.

**A** l ________ ttle

**B** f ________ nny

**C** love ________

2 Which word rhymes with **Sam**?

**A** sat

**B** dam

**C** mad

3 Which word rhymes with **kiss**?

**A** kissed

**B** his

**C** miss

4 Unscramble the letters to make words from the text.

**A** ssik ________

**B** lovse ________

**C** fnnyu ________

5 Say the word. How many sounds can you hear?

**A** kiss ________

**B** is ________

**C** Sam ________

## Vocabulary

6 Which word does **not** belong?

**A** Lindy

**B** funny

**C** little

## Grammar

7 Write a noun on the line.

Little ________

## Punctuation

8 Write the sentence correctly on the lines.

| Lindy | a sister. | has |
|---|---|---|

________

________

________

## Reading and Comprehension

# Run

We like to run. We run with our dog. His name is Red. Red runs fast.

1. Circle the correct word from the text.

   Red runs ______________.

   **A** can

   **B** children

   **C** fast

2. Circle the sentence that matches the picture.

   **A** They can run.

   **B** Red and a dog can run.

   **C** Here is a dog.

3. Write a word from the text.

   His ______________ is Red.

4. Write a word from the text.

   We like to ______________.

5. Draw something Red can do.

6. Is Red fun?

   ☐ yes

   ☐ no

## Spelling

1 Write the missing letters to make words from the text.

A r ________ n

B f ________ st

C R ________ d

2 Which word rhymes with **run**?

A running

B fun

C rug

3 Which word rhymes with **Red**?

A bed

B run

C pet

4 Unscramble the letters to make words from the text.

A rnu ________

B fats ________

C mane ________

5 Say the word. How many sounds can you hear?

A run ________

B like ________

C Red ________

## Vocabulary

6 Which word does **not** belong?

A run

B stop

C jump

## Grammar

7 Write a noun on the line.

________

## Punctuation

8 Write the sentence correctly on the lines.

| Red | run. | can |
|---|---|---|

________

________

________

## Reading and Comprehension

# Vet

On Wednesday we took our Coco to see the vet. The vet has a good job.

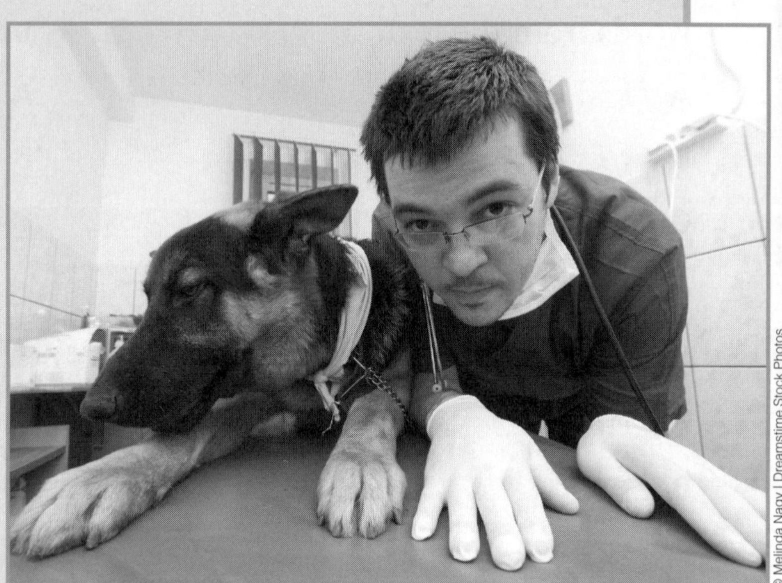

© Melinda Nagy | Dreamstime Stock Photos

1 Circle the correct word from the text.
The dog went to see the

................................................................ .

**A** pet

**B** dog

**C** vet

2 Circle the words that match the picture.

**A** our dog and the vet

**B** our dog

**C** Wednesday

3 Write a word from the text.

The vet has a good

................................................................ .

4 Write a word from the text.

The dog saw the vet on

................................................................ .

5 Draw something a vet can help.

6 Does the vet like his job?

☐ yes

☐ no

## Spelling

1 Write the missing letters to make words from the text.

**A** v ________ t

**B** too ________

**C** jo ________

2 Which word rhymes with **vet**?

**A** van

**B** pet

**C** dog

3 Which word rhymes with **took**?

**A** tool

**B** take

**C** book

4 Unscramble the letters to make words from the text.

**A** koot ________

**B** ees ________

**C** boj ________

5 Say the word. How many sounds can you hear?

**A** vet ________

**B** took ________

**C** job ________

## Vocabulary

6 Which word does **not** belong?

**A** Wednesday

**B** Sunday

**C** sun

## Grammar

7 Write a proper noun on the line.

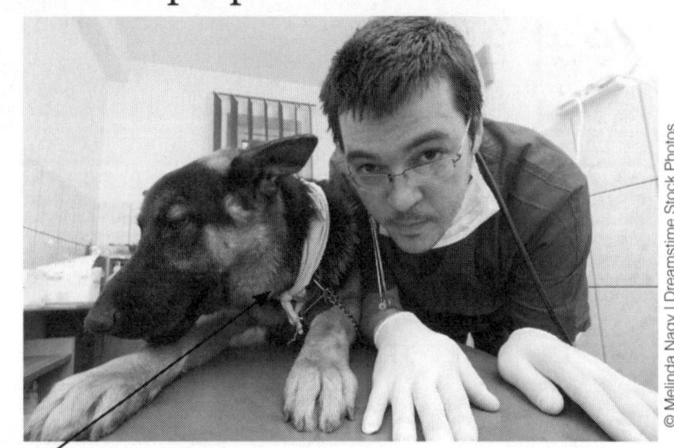



________________________

## Punctuation

8 Write the sentence correctly on the lines.

| has | a good job. | A vet |
|---|---|---|

________________________

________________________

________________________

## Reading and Comprehension

# Spider

One spider sat in its web. It was hungry. It needed food. It needed to eat a bug.

1 Circle the correct word from the text.

The spider was ..................................................

**A** food

**B** web

**C** hungry

2 Circle the words that match the picture.

**A** one hungry spider

**B** one web

**C** a spider and a bug

3 Write a word from the text.

One spider .................................................. in its web.

4 Write a word from the text.

The spider needed to eat a ...................................................

5 Draw something that might happen next in the text.

6 Do you want the spider to eat a bug?

☐ yes

☐ no

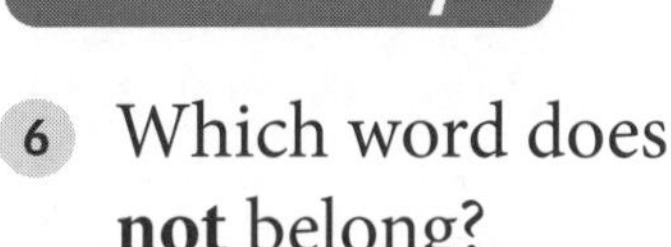

## Spelling

1 Write the missing letters to make words from the text.

A w ______ b

B on ______

C b ______ g

2 Which word rhymes with **sat**?

A sit

B web

C pat

3 Which word rhymes with **bug**?

A grub

B mug

C web

4 Unscramble the letters to make words from the text.

A tea ______

B gub ______

C bew ______

5 Say the word. How many sounds can you hear?

A bug ______

B web ______

C sat ______

## Vocabulary

6 Which word does **not** belong?

A bug

B ant

C web

## Grammar

7 Write a noun on the line.

______

## Punctuation

8 Write the sentence correctly on the lines.

needed | It | a bug.

______

______

______

## Reading and Comprehension

# Yum!

Yum! We made banana muffins on Sunday. They were good. I ate three.

1. Circle the correct word from the text.

   We made ………………………… on Sunday.

   **A** banana

   **B** good

   **C** muffins

2. Circle the words that match the picture.

   **A** banana muffin

   **B** banana muffins

   **C** a yummy muffin

3. Write a word from the text.

   They were ………………………… .

4. Write a word from the text.

   We made ………………………… muffins.

5. Draw something that might happen next in the text.

6. Does the writer like bananas?

   ☐ yes

   ☐ no

UNIT 23B

## Spelling

1 Write the missing letters to make words from the text.

A goo ________

B g ________ ________ d

C mad ________

2 Which word rhymes with **yum**?

A yummy

B yes

C hum

3 Which word rhymes with **made**?

A make

B wade

C web

4 Unscramble the letters to make words from the text.

A maed ________

B muy ________

C muinsff ________

5 Say the word. How many sounds can you hear?

A made ________

B yum ________

C good ________

## Vocabulary

6 Which word does **not** belong?

A yum

B yummy

C yuck

## Grammar

7 Adjectives can describe a noun. Write an adjective.

The muffins were

________________.

## Punctuation

8 Write the sentence correctly on the lines.

| We | muffins. | made |
|---|---|---|

________________

________________

________________

# Reading and Comprehension

Add a word from the box to each sentence.

| sisters | Kangaroos | jump | help |
|---|---|---|---|

1 Here are two ____________________.

2 ____________________ can jump.

3 Nine children can ____________________.

4 Mum can ____________________ Nan.

Add a word from the box to each sentence.

| run | vet | good | web |
|---|---|---|---|

© creativecommons stockphotos | Dreamstime Stock Photos

5 The spider sat in a ____________________.

6 Muffins are ____________________!

7 The dog can ____________________ fast.

© Melinda Nagy | Dreamstime Stock Photos

8 The ____________________ has a good job.

## Spelling, Vocabulary, Grammar and Punctuation

Write the missing words.
Using a different colour for each word, colour in the letters that make the words.

| | | | | | |
|---|---|---|---|---|---|
| 9 | © creativecommons stockphotos \| Dreamstime Stock Photos | One spider sat in a ___ ___ ___. | r | i | k |
| 10 | | ___ ___ ___! I love muffins. | v | w | t |
| 11 | | Nan has ___ ___ ___ on the computer. | w | oo | ss |
| 12 | | The dog can ___ ___ ___ fast. | f | e | b |
| 13 | | Here are ___ ___ ___ kangaroos. | l | e | m |
| 14 | | They ___ ___ ___ ___ happy. | Y | u | o |
| 15 | | Lindy loves to ___ ___ ___ ___ Sam. | t | u | n |
| 16 | © Melinda Nagy \| Dreamstime Stock Photos | The ___ ___ ___ has a good job. | k | u | n |

## Reading

# Scarlet and Kangaroo

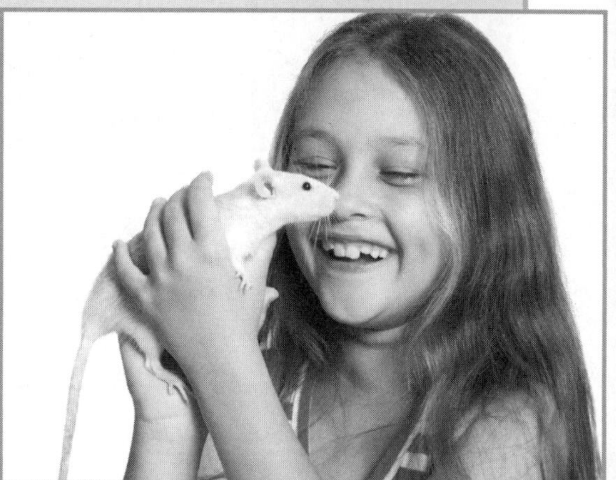

My sister, Scarlet, has a pet rat. Its name is Kangaroo. It loves to run and jump. It can run fast. I help my sister give it food. It is a fun job. A rat is a good pet.

By Hamish

1 The rat's name is

- **A** Kangaroo.
- **B** Sister.
- **C** Rat.

2 The rat runs

- **A** jumps.
- **B** pet.
- **C** fast.

3 A rat is

- **A** my sister.
- **B** a fun job.
- **C** a good pet.

4 How many rats are there?

- **A** three
- **B** two
- **C** one

5 The rat's name is Kangaroo because it can jump.

- **A** yes
- **B** no

6 Does Scarlet think a rat is a good pet?

- **A** yes
- **B** no

## Spelling

1 Write the missing letters to make words from the text.

A r ___ t B j ___ mp C h ___ lp

2 Which word rhymes with **pet**?

A get B ten C pen

3 Which word rhymes with **fun**?

A fan B run C fat

4 Unscramble the letters to make words from the text.

A nmae ______________________

B pumj ______________________

C tasf ______________________

5 Say the word. How many sounds can you hear?

A name ______________________

B jump ______________________

C food ______________________

## Vocabulary

6 Which word does **not** belong?

A sad B fun C happy

## Grammar

7 Write a proper noun on each line.

A ______________________

B ______________________

## Punctuation

8 Write the sentence correctly on the line.

| a good pet. | A rat | is |

## Reading and Comprehension

# Foxy

Foxy is our cat.

Foxy likes to play in boxes. He likes to jump out of boxes. Boo!

1 Circle the correct word from the text.

Foxy is in a ______________.

- **A** boat
- **B** box
- **C** cat

2 Circle the sentence that matches the picture.

- **A** The cat can sit.
- **B** We like to play.
- **C** Foxy plays in boxes.

3 Write a word from the text.

Foxy is a ______________.

4 Write a word from the text.

Foxy likes to

______________

out of boxes.

5 Draw what might happen next in the text.

6 Why does Foxy play in boxes?

- **A** It is a box.
- **B** It is fun.
- **C** Foxy jumps out of boxes.

## Spelling

1 Write the missing letters to make words from the text.

A bo ..........

B Fo .......... y

C pla ..........

2 Circle the word that rhymes with **play**.

A boxes

B day

C plop

3 Circle the word that rhymes with **box**.

A likes

B fox

C us

4 Unscramble the letters to make words from the text.

A xob ..........

B plya ..........

C tuo ..........

5 Say the word. How many sounds can you hear?

A box ..........

B Foxy ..........

C likes ..........

## Vocabulary

6 Which word does **not** belong?

A play

B fun

C stop

## Grammar

7 Choose the verb from the box to complete the sentence.

| jumps | cat | box |
|---|---|---|

Foxy .......... out.

## Punctuation

8 Write the sentence correctly on the lines. Begin with a capital letter and end with a full stop.

| to play | Foxy | likes |
|---|---|---|

..........

..........

..........

## Reading and Comprehension

# Zed

The letter Zed is for zero, zip, zipper, zoo, zoom. My favourite Zed word is zebra. Zebras are black and white.

By Zoe

© Luca Olivieri | Dreamstime Stock Photos

1 Zed is a ______________.

- **A** zero
- **B** zebra
- **C** letter

2 Circle the word that matches the picture.

- **A** zebra
- **B** zipper
- **C** Zed

3 Write a word from the text.

Zebras are black and

______________.

4 Write a word from the text.

Add *m* to zoo to make

______________.

5 Does the writer like zebras?

☐ yes

☐ no

6 Why is zebra Zoe's favourite Zed word?

- **A** It is her favourite animal.
- **B** It is black and white.
- **C** A zebra can zoom.

## Spelling

1 Write the missing letters to make words from the text.

**A** Z ________ d

**B** zer ________

**C** z ________ p

2 Circle the word that rhymes with **zip**.

**A** zap

**B** zit

**C** pip

3 Circle the word that rhymes with **white**.

**A** which

**B** kite

**C** when

4 Unscramble the letters to make words from the text.

**A** zeor ________

**B** ooz ________

**C** mooz ________

5 Say the word. How many sounds can you hear?

**A** zoo ________

**B** zoom ________

**C** black ________

## Vocabulary

6 Which word does **not** belong?

**A** black

**B** white

**C** zebra

## Grammar

7 Adjectives can describe a noun. Write adjectives.

Zebras are ________

and ________.

## Punctuation

8 Write the sentence correctly on the lines. Begin with a capital letter and end with a full stop.

| for zero | is | Zed |
|---|---|---|

________

________

________

## Reading and Comprehension

# Quick

QUICK—emu

Not quick—snail

QUACK—duck

Not quack—elephant

QUIET—snake

Not quiet—rooster

SHHH!

1 The ______________ is not quick.

- **A** snail
- **B** duck
- **C** emu

2 Circle the word that matches the emu.

- **A** quiet
- **B** quick
- **C** quack

3 Write a word from the text.

"Quack," said the ______________.

4 Write a word from the text.

The snake is ______________.

5 Does an elephant say "Quack"?

- ☐ yes
- ☐ no

6 What does the boy want?

- **A** quiet
- **B** quack
- **C** quick

## Spelling

1 Write the missing letters to make words from the text.

**A** ______ ______ ick

**B** ______ ______ ack

**C** qui ______ t

2 Circle the word that rhymes with **quick**.

**A** stuck

**B** stick

**C** stack

3 Circle the word that rhymes with **snake**.

**A** cake

**B** snail

**C** snack

4 Unscramble the letters to make words from the text.

**A** qucki ______________

**B** qucka ______________

**C** udck ______________

5 Say the word. How many sounds can you hear?

**A** duck ______________

**B** quick ______________

**C** snake ______________

## Vocabulary

6 Which word does **not** belong?

**A** kookaburra

**B** duck

**C** quiet

## Grammar

7 Choose a conjunction from the box to complete the sentence.

| or | and | but | so | because |
|---|---|---|---|---|

Ducks quack

______________________________

elephants do not quack.

## Punctuation

8 Write the sentence correctly on the lines. Begin with a capital letter and end with a full stop.

| a snail | quick | is not |
|---|---|---|

______________________________

______________________________

______________________________

## Reading and Comprehension

# Do this! Don't do that!

Stop!

Go!

Keep off the grass.

Keep off the garden.

Keep quiet.

Walk.

Don't walk.

Follow the rules.

1. Keep ______ the garden.
   - **A** off
   - **B** to
   - **C** on

2. Circle the sentence that matches the picture.
   - **A** Walk.
   - **B** Keep quiet.
   - **C** Keep off.

3. Write a word from the text.

   Follow the ______.

4. Write a word from the text.

   ______ off the grass.

5. Can you play in the garden?
   - ☐ yes
   - ☐ no

6. Why are rules good?
   - **A** They keep you off the garden.
   - **B** They keep you quiet.
   - **C** They keep you safe.

## Spelling

1 Write the missing letters to make words from the text.

A St ________ p!

B G ________ !

C Wal ________ .

2 Circle the word that rhymes with **walk**.

A grass

B talk

C wall

3 Circle the word that rhymes with **keep**.

A keen

B deep

C kelp

4 Unscramble the letters to make words from the text.

A wlka ________

B ssgra ________

C ruels ________

5 Say the word. How many sounds can you hear?

A stop ________

B walk ________

C keep ________

## Vocabulary

6 Which word does **not** belong?

A walk

B go

C don't

## Grammar

7 Choose a conjunction from the box to complete the sentence.

| or | and | but | so | because |
|---|---|---|---|---|

Keep off the grass

________

keep out of the garden.

## Punctuation

8 Write the question correctly on the lines. Begin with a capital letter and end with a question mark.

| the rules | you | can follow |
|---|---|---|

________

________

________

## Reading and Comprehension

# Thank you

Dear Dad

Thank you for the book. I got it yesterday. Mum is helping me read it. I love it because it is funny. I love the pictures best.

Love

Jasmine

1. Circle the correct word from the text.

   I .......................... it yesterday.

   **A** love

   **B** got

   **C** book

2. Circle the word or words that match the picture.

   **A** Jasmine

   **B** book

   **C** Dear Dad

3. Write a word from the text.

   Jasmine loves the book because it is .......................... .

4. Write a word from the text.

   Mum is helping me .......................... it.

5. Is Dad helping Jasmine read the book?

   ☐ yes

   ☐ no

6. What does Jasmine like best about the book?

   **A** It is from Dad.

   **B** She loves the pictures best.

   **C** It is funny.

## Spelling

1 Write the missing letters to make words from the text.

A f ________ nny

B b ________ st

C l ________ ve

2 Circle the word that rhymes with **book**.

A boot

B boom

C took

3 Circle the word that rhymes with **best**.

A test

B beast

C bees

4 Unscramble the letters to make words from the text.

A koob ________

B thkan ________

C inghepl ________

5 Say the word. How many sounds can you hear?

A book ________

B thank ________

C love ________

## Vocabulary

6 Which word does **not** belong?

A Jasmine

B Dad

C pictures

## Grammar

7 Choose a conjunction from the box to complete the sentence.

| or | and | but | so | because |
|---|---|---|---|---|

I love it

________________________

it is funny.

## Punctuation

8 Write the sentence correctly on the lines. Begin with a capital letter and end with a full stop.

| for | the book | thank you |
|---|---|---|

________________________

________________________

________________________

## Reading and Comprehension

# Please

Please wash your hands before you eat. Wash them with soap. Get rid of germs.

1 Circle the correct word from the text.

Wash your ____________

before you eat.

**A** head

**B** soap

**C** hands

2 Circle the sentence that matches the picture.

**A** Please wish your hands.

**B** Please wash your hand.

**C** Please wash your hands.

3 Write a word from the text.

Wash them with

____________.

4 Write a word from the text.

Get rid of

____________.

5 Do you wash your hands before lunch?

☐ yes

☐ no

6 Why should you use soap?

**A** to get rid of germs

**B** to wash hands

**C** to smell good

## Spelling

1 Write the missing letters to make words from the text.

A w ______ sh

B h ______ nds

C so ______ p

2 Circle the word that rhymes with **rid**.

A ripe

B lid

C rip

3 Circle the word that rhymes with **get**.

A gate

B great

C set

4 Unscramble the letters to make words from the text.

A pleesa ______

B hadns ______

C wsha ______

5 Say the word. How many sounds can you hear?

A wash ______

B please ______

C soap ______

## Vocabulary

6 Which word does **not** belong?

A wash

B germs

C soap

## Grammar

7 Choose a conjunction from the box to complete the sentence.

| or | and | but | so | because |
|---|---|---|---|---|

Wash your hands

______

you can eat.

## Punctuation

8 Write the question correctly on the lines. Begin with a capital letter and end with a question mark.

| with soap | wash | did you |
|---|---|---|

______

______

______

______

## Reading and Comprehension

# Recycle

At my house we recycle.

We recycle:

paper

glass

cans

and plastic.

We recycle food scraps too. We give food scraps to our worms.

By Greta

1. Circle the word from the text.

   At my house we ______________.

   **A** recycle

   **B** paper

   **C** glass

2. Circle the word or words that match the picture.

   **A** recycling

   **B** glass and cans

   **C** food scraps for worms

3. Write a word from the text.
   We give food scraps to our

   ______________.

4. Write a word from the text.

   Worms eat ______________.

5. Does Greta recycle bottles?

   ☐ yes

   ☐ no

6. What do worms like to eat?

   **A** glass

   **B** food scraps

   **C** plastic

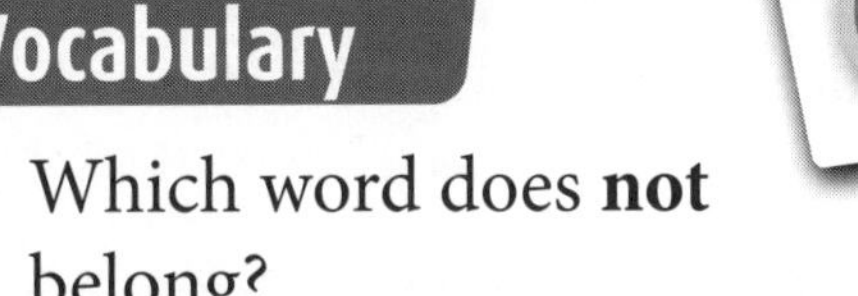


## Spelling

1 Write the missing letters to make words from the text.

A foo ____

B scr ____ ps

C p ____ per

2 Circle the word that rhymes with **give**.

A gave

B given

C live

3 Circle the word that rhymes with **house**.

A hose

B mouse

C use

4 Unscramble the letters to make words from the text.

A huose ____

B doof ____

C worsm ____

5 Say the word. How many sounds can you hear?

A house ____

B glass ____

C food ____

## Vocabulary

6 Which word does **not** belong?

A glass

B plastic

C worms

## Grammar

7 Choose a conjunction from the box to complete the sentence.

| or | and | but | so | because |
|---|---|---|---|---|

We recycle glass

____

we recycle cans.

## Punctuation

8 Write the question correctly on the lines. Begin with a capital letter and end with a question mark.

do you | food scraps | recycle

____

____

____

## Reading and Comprehension

Add a word from the box to each sentence.

| Zebras | boxes | Quack | Keep |
|---|---|---|---|

1 Please Keep off the grass  ______________ off the grass.

2 A duck says, "______________".

3 ______________ are black and white.

4 The cat likes to hide in ______________.

Add a word from the box to each sentence.

| book | eat | soap | paper |
|---|---|---|---|

5 Recycle all your ______________.

6 PLEASE WASH YOUR HANDS  Wash your hands with ______________!

7 Mum is helping Jasmine read a ______________.

8 PLEASE WASH YOUR HANDS  Wash your hands before you ______________.

## Spelling, Vocabulary, Grammar and Punctuation

Complete the missing words.
Using a different colour for each word, colour in the letters that make the words.

| | | | | | |
|---|---|---|---|---|---|
| 9 | | A cat jumped out of the ___ ___ ___. | i | e | x |
| 10 | | Fast cars can z___ ___ ___. | a | n | s |
| 11 | | An emu is qu___ ___ ___. | n | s | d |
| 12 | | Some books are fu___ ___ ___. | p | s | r |
| 13 | PLEASE WASH YOUR HANDS | W___ ___ ___ your hands. | o | i | k |
| 14 | PLEASE WASH YOUR HANDS | Get ___ ___ ___ of germs. | b | o | h |
| 15 | | Recycle gl___ ___ ___. | r | c | y |
| 16 | | Recycle pa___ ___ ___. | a | o | m |

Reading

NAPLAN-STYLE 4 READING TEST

## Heading

At my school we have rules. We have to keep quiet at reading time. We have to read every day. We have to recycle everything. We must keep off the garden.

I like rules. They help everyone stay safe and happy.

By Nathan

1 At school there are __________.

- A quiet
- B recycle
- C rules

2 Children read every __________.

- A day
- B where
- C time

3 Children must keep __________ the garden.

- A on
- B in
- C off

4 The school recycles __________.

- A some things
- B everything
- C nothing

5 Rules keep children safe.

- ☐ yes
- ☐ no

6 Does Nathan follow the rules?

- ☐ yes
- ☐ no

NAPLAN-STYLE 4 CONVENTIONS OF LANGUAGE TEST

## Spelling

1 Write the missing letters to make words from the text.

**A** rul ___ s **B** saf ___ **C** happ ___

2 Circle the word that rhymes with **like**.

**A** love **B** help **C** bike

3 Circle the word that rhymes with **must**.

**A** rust **B** music **C** fast

4 Unscramble the letters to make words from the text.

**A** scoolh ..................

**B** ruesl ..................

**C** dera ..................

5 Say the words. How many sounds can you hear?

**A** read ..................

**B** school ..................

**C** safe ..................

## Vocabulary

6 Which word does **not** belong?

**A** safe **B** garden **C** happy

## Grammar

7 Write words or a sentence to match the picture.

______________________

## Punctuation

8 Write the sentence correctly on the line.

| Nathan | every day | reads |
|---|---|---|

Reprinted 2019, 2020, 2021, 2023

**Updated in 2025 for the NSW Curriculum and Australian Curriculum Version 9.0 changes**

ISBN 978 1 74125 608 6

Pascal Press
PO Box 250
Glebe NSW 2037
www.pascalpress.com.au

Publisher: Vivienne Joannou
Project editor: Rosemary Peers
Edited by Rosemary Peers
Proofread by Barbara Bessant
Answers checked by Glenda Walsh
Cover and page design by Kim Webber
Typeset by Julianne Billington (lj Design) and Leanne Richters (Grizzly Graphics)
Printed by Vivar Printing/Green Giant Press